Oh, So Cute Doll Clothes ™

Contents

Pretty Lace

THREAD
SKILL LEVEL

◼◼☐☐
EASY

FINISHED SIZES
Instructions given fit small 8-inch chubby doll; changes for medium 10-inch cloth doll and large 12-inch cloth doll are in [ ].

FINISHED MEASUREMENTS
Chest: 8½ inches *(small)* [8½ inches *(medium)*, 9 inches *(large)*]

MATERIALS
- Size 10 crochet cotton: 350 yds white
- Size steel crochet hook needed for size or size needed to obtain gauge
- Sewing needle
- ¼-inch buttons: 2 white
- Dark pink ribbon:
  ¼-inch-wide: 1½ yds
  ⅛-inch-wide: 1 yd
- ½-inch-wide flower appliqués: 20
- White sewing thread

GAUGE
Small & Medium Sizes: Size 7/1.65mm steel crochet hook: 15 dc = 2 inches; 8 dc rows = 2 inches

Large Size: Size 6/1.80 steel crochet hook: 13 dc = 2 inches; 7 dc rows = 2 inches

PATTERN NOTES
Join with slip stitch as indicated unless otherwise stated.

Chain-3 at beginning of row or round counts as first double crochet unless otherwise stated.

Chain-4 at beginning of row or round counts as first double crochet and chain-1 space.

SPECIAL STITCH
Shell: (2 dc, ch 2, 2 dc) in designated place.

INSTRUCTIONS
DRESS
Row 1: Starting at neck, ch 41, sc in 2nd ch from hook and in each ch across, turn. *(40 sc)*

Row 2: Ch 3 *(see Pattern Notes)*, dc in same st, dc in next st, [2 dc in next st, dc in next st] across, turn. *(60 dc)*

Row 3: Ch 3, dc in same st, dc in each of next 2 sts, [2 dc in next st, dc in each of next 2 sts] across, turn. *(80 dc)*

Row 4: Ch 3, dc in same st, dc in each of next 3 sts, [2 dc in next st, dc in each of next 3 sts] across, turn. *(100 dc)*

Row 5: Ch 3, dc in each of next 13 sts, for **armhole**, ch 5, sk next 22 sts, dc in each of next 28 sts, for **armhole**, ch 5, sk next 22 sts, dc in each of last 14 sts, turn. *(56 dc, 10 chs)*

Row 6: Ch 1, sc in each dc and ch across, turn. *(66 sc)*

Row 7: For **skirt**, ch 3, (dc, ch 2, dc) in next st, [sk next st, (dc, ch 2, dc) in next st] across, turn. *(33 ch-2 sps)*

Rows 8–17 [8–17, 8–19]: Ch 3, **shell** *(see Special Stitch)* in each ch-2 sp across, dc in last st, turn. Fasten off at end of last row. *(33 shells, 2 dc)*

NECK EDGING (OPTIONAL)
Working in starting ch on opposite side of row 1, **join** *(see Pattern Notes)* in first ch, ch 3, [sk next ch, shell in next ch across to last ch, dc in last ch. Fasten off.

SLEEVES
Rnd 1: Join with sc around last dc before ch-5 on 1 armhole in row 5, hdc around same dc, working across 22 sk sts, dc in each of next 9 dc, 2 dc in next st, dc in each of next 2 sts, 2 dc in next st, dc in each of next 9 dc, hdc around next dc in row 5, sc around same dc, working in opposite side of ch-5, sl st in each ch across, join in beg sc. *(33 sts)*

Rnd 2: Ch 1, sc in first st, hdc in next st, dc in each of next 24 sts, hdc in next st, sc in next st, sc in each of next 2 sl sts, sk next sl st, sc in each of last 2 sl sts, join in beg sc. *(32 sts)*

Rnd 3: Ch 1, sc in first st, hdc in next st, [**dc dec** *(see Stitch Guide)* in next 2 sts] 12 times, hdc in next st, sc in each of last 5 sts, join in beg sc. (20 sts)

Rnd 4: Ch 1, sc in each st around, join in beg sc. *(20 sc)*

Rnd 5: Ch 3, (dc, ch 2, 2 dc) in same st, sk next st, [shell in next st, sk next st] around, join in 3rd ch of beg ch-3. Fasten off.

Rep on other armhole.

RIGHT PLACKET
Row 1: With WS facing, join with sc in bottom right-hand corner, working up to neck edge in ends of rows, evenly sp sc across to neck edge with 2 sc in end of each dc row, turn.

Row 2: Ch 1, sc in first st, for **buttonhole**, ch 3, sk next st, sc in each of next 5 sts, for **buttonhole**, ch 3, sk next st, sc in each st across. Fasten off.

LEFT PLACKET
Row 1: With WS facing, join with sc in top left-hand corner at neck edge, working down to hem edge in ends of rows, evenly sp sc across to hem edge with 2 sc in end of each dc row, turn.

Row 2: Ch 1, sc in each st across. Fasten off.

Sew buttons to Left Placket opposite buttonholes.

Sew 2 appliqués to center front of bodice above shells.

Sew 1 appliqué to each bottom corner of skirt, sew remaining appliqués in pairs evenly spaced around bottom edge of skirt *(see photo)*.

BONNET
Rnd 1: Ch 6, join in beg ch to form ring, **ch 4**, *(see Pattern Notes)*, [dc in ring, ch 1] 9 times, join in 3rd ch of beg ch-4. *(10 dc, 10 ch sps)*

Rnd 2: Sl st in next ch sp, ch 4, dc in same sp, (dc, ch 1, dc) in each ch sp around, join in 3rd ch of beg ch-4. *(20 dc, 10 ch sps)*

Rnd 3: Sl st in next ch sp, ch 3, (dc, ch 2, 2 dc) in same sp, shell in each ch sp around, join in 3rd ch of beg ch-3. *(10 shells)*

Rnd 4: Sl st in next dc, sl st in next ch sp, ch 3, (dc, ch 2, 2 dc) in same sp, shell in each ch sp around, join in 3rd ch of beg ch-3, **do not turn**.

Row 5: Now working in rows, ch 3, shell in each of next 9 ch sps, sk next dc, dc in next dc, leaving rem sts unworked, turn. *(9 shells)*

Rows 6–10: Ch 3, shell in ch sp of each of next 9 shells, dc in last st, turn.

Rows 11 & 12: Ch 4, [(3 dc, ch 3, 3 dc) in ch sp of next shell, ch 1] across, dc in last st, turn. Fasten off at end of last row.

For **ties**, weave 1 yd of ¼-inch-wide ribbon through shells of row 11, pull ends even.

NECK EDGING

Row 1: Join with sc at one side of neck edge, evenly sp sts, work 21 sc across to opposite end of neck edge, turn. *(22 sc)*

Row 2: Ch 1, sc in each st across. Fasten off.

SHOE
MAKE 2.

Rnd 1: Ch 10, dc in 4th ch from hook *(first 3 chs count as first dc)*, dc in each of next 5 chs, 5 dc in last ch, working on opposite side of ch, dc in each of next 5 chs, 2 dc in last ch, join in 3rd ch of beg ch-3. *(19 dc)*

Rnd 2: Ch 3, dc in same st, dc in each of next 6 sts, 2 dc in each of next 5 sts, dc in each of next 6 sts, 2 dc in last st, join in 3rd ch of beg ch-3. *(26 dc)*

Rnd 3: Ch 3, dc in each st around, join in 3rd ch of beg ch-3

Rnd 4: Ch 3, dc in each of next 8 sts, [dc dec in each of next 2 sts] 4 times, dc in each of last 9 sts, join in 3rd ch of beg ch-3. *(22 dc)*

Rnd 5: Ch 1, sc in each of first 9 sts, [sc dec in next 2 sts] twice, sc in each of last 9 sts, join in beg sc. Fasten off. *(20 sts)*

Weave 12 inches of ¼-inch-wide ribbon through stitches of row 4 at heel, pull ends even and tie around ankle with bow at front.

Sew 1 appliqué to toe.

PANTS

Rnd 1: Ch 60, sl st in first ch to form ring, ch 3, dc in each ch around, join in 3rd ch of beg ch-3. *(60 dc)*

Rnd 2: Ch 3, dc in each of next 4 sts, 2 dc in next st, [dc in each of next 5 sts, 2 dc in next st] around, join in 3rd ch of beg ch-3. *(70 dc)*

Rnds 3–4 [3–6, 3–9]: Ch 3, dc in each st around, join in 3rd ch of beg ch-3.

Rnd 5 [7, 10]: Ch 3, dc in each st around, join in 3rd ch of beg ch-3, ch 6, sk next 34 sts, sl st in next st. Fasten off.

LEGS

Rnd 1: Join in 4th ch of ch-6, ch 3, dc in next ch, dc dec in next ch and st, dc in each st across to one st before opposite side of ch-6, dc dec in next st and next ch, dc in each of last 2 chs, join in 3rd ch of beg ch-3. *(40 sts)*

Rnd 0 [2, 2]: Ch 3, dc in each st around, join in 3rd ch of beg ch-3.

Rnd 2 [3, 3]: Ch 1, **sc dec** *(see Stitch Guide)* in first 2 sts [sc dec in next 2 sts], around, join in beg sc dec. *(20 sts)*

Rnd 3 [4, 4]: Ch 1, sc in each st around, join in beg sc. *(20 sc)*

Rnd 4 [5, 5]: Ch 3, (dc, ch 2, 2 dc) in same st, sk next st, [shell in next st, sk next st] around, join in 3rd ch of beg ch-3. Fasten off. *(10 shells)*

Working on opposite side of ch-6, rep on other Leg opening.

Cut ⅛-inch-wide ribbon in half, weave 1 strand ribbon through first rnd of sts on front and weave other strand ribbon through first rnd of sts on back.

Pull ribbon ends even, tie ends in bow at each side of Pants.

YARN
SKILL LEVEL

EASY

FINISHED SIZE
Fits 10-inch chubby doll

FINISHED MEASUREMENT
Chest: 11 inches

MATERIALS
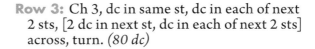

- Super fine (fingering) yarn:
  2 oz/350 yds/57g white
- Size C/2/2.75mm crochet hook
  or size needed to obtain gauge
- Sewing needle
- ⅜-inch buttons:
  2 white
- ⅛-inch-wide dark pink ribbon:
  2½ yds
- ½-inch-wide flower appliqués:
  24
- White sewing thread

GAUGE
6 dc = 1 inch; 5 dc rows = 1½ inches

PATTERN NOTES
Join with slip stitch as indicated unless
   otherwise stated.

Chain-3 at beginning of row or round counts as
   first double crochet unless otherwise stated.

Chain 4 at beginning of row or round counts as
   first double crochet and chain-1 space.

SPECIAL STITCH
Shell: (2 dc, ch 2, 2 dc) in designated place.

INSTRUCTIONS
DRESS
Row 1: Starting at neck, ch 41, sc in 2nd ch from
   hook and in each ch across, turn. *(40 sc)*

Row 2: Ch 3 *(see Pattern Notes)*, dc in same
   st, dc in next st, [2 dc in next st, dc in next st]
   across, turn. *(60 dc)*

Row 3: Ch 3, dc in same st, dc in each of next
   2 sts, [2 dc in next st, dc in each of next 2 sts]
   across, turn. *(80 dc)*

Row 4: Ch 3, dc in same st, dc in each of next
   3 sts, [2 dc in next st, dc in each of next 3 sts]
   across, turn. *(100 dc)*

Row 5: Ch 3, dc in each of next 13 sts, for
   armhole, ch 5, sk next 22 sts, dc in each of next
   28 sts, for **armhole**, ch 5, sk next 22 sts, dc in
   each of last 14 sts, turn. *(56 dc, 10 chs)*

Row 6: Ch 1, sc in each dc and ch across,
   turn. *(66 sc)*

Row 7: For **skirt**, ch 3, (dc, ch 2, dc) in next st,
   [sk next st, (dc, ch 2, dc) in next st] across, turn.
   (33 ch-2 sps)

Rows 8–17: Ch 3, **shell** *(see Special Stitch)* in
   each ch-2 sp across, dc in last st, turn. Fasten
   off at end of last row. *(33 shells, 2 dc)*

SLEEVES
Rnd 1: Join with sc around last dc before ch-5
   on 1 armhole in row 5, hdc around same dc,
   working across 22 sk sts, dc in each of next 9
   dc, 2 dc in next st, dc in each of next 2 sts, 2 dc
   in next st, dc in each of next 9 dc, hdc around
   next dc in row 5, sc around same dc, working in
   opposite side of ch-5, sl st in each ch across, join
   in beg sc. *(33 sts)*

Rnd 2: Ch 1, sc in first st, hdc in next st, dc in
   each of next 24 sts, hdc in next st, sc in next st,
   sc in each of next 2 sl sts, sk next sl st, sc in each
   of last 2 sl sts, join in beg sc. *(32 sts)*

Rnd 3: Ch 1, sc in first st, hdc in next st, [**dc dec** *(see
   Stitch Guide)* in next 2 sts] 12 times, hdc in next st,
   sc in each of last 5 sts, join in beg sc. *(20 sts)*

Rnd 4: Ch 1, sc in each st around, join in beg
   sc. *(20 sc)*

Rnd 5: Ch 3, (dc, ch 2, 2 dc) in same st, sk next
   st, [shell in next st, sk next st] around, join in
   3rd ch of beg ch-3. Fasten off.

Rep on other armhole.

RIGHT PLACKET

Row 1: With WS facing, join with sc in bottom right-hand corner, working up to neck edge in ends of rows, evenly sp sc across to neck edge with 2 sc in end of each dc row, turn.

Row 2: Ch 1, sc in first st, for **buttonhole**, ch 3, sk next st, sc in each of next 5 sts, for **buttonhole**, ch 3, sk next st, sc in each st across. Fasten off.

LEFT PLACKET

Row 1: With WS facing, join with sc in top left-hand corner at neck edge, working down to hem edge in ends of rows, evenly sp sc across to hem edge with 2 sc in end of each dc row, turn.

Row 2: Ch 1, sc in each st across. Fasten off.

Sew buttons to Left Placket opposite buttonholes.

Sew 2 appliqués to center front of bodice above shells.

Sew remaining appliqués in pairs evenly sp around bottom edge of skirt (*see photo*).

BONNET

Rnd 1: Ch 6, join in beg ch to form ring, **ch 4**, (*see Pattern Notes*), [dc in ring, ch 1] 9 times, join in 3rd ch of beg ch-4. (*10 dc, 10 ch sps*)

Rnd 2: Sl st in next ch sp, ch 4, dc in same sp, (dc, ch 1, dc) in each ch sp around, join in 3rd ch of beg ch-4. (*20 dc, 10 ch sps*)

Rnd 3: Sl st in next ch sp, ch 3, (dc, ch 2, 2 dc) in same sp, shell in each ch sp around, join in 3rd ch of beg ch-3. (*10 shells*)

Rnd 4: Sl st in next dc, sl st in next ch sp, ch 3, (dc, ch 2, 2 dc) in same sp, shell in each ch sp around, join in 3rd ch of beg ch-3, **do not turn.**

Row 5: Now working in rows, ch 3, shell in each of next 9 ch sps, sk next dc, dc in next dc, leaving rem sts unworked, turn. (*9 shells*)

Rows 6–10: Ch 3, shell in ch sp of each of next 9 shells, dc in last st, turn.

Rows 11 & 12: Ch 4, [(3 dc, ch 3, 3 dc) in ch sp of next shell, ch 1] across, dc in last st. Fasten off at end of last row.

For **ties**, weave 1 yd of ribbon through shells of row 11, pull ends even.

NECK EDGING

Row 1: Join with sc at one side of neck edge, evenly sp sts, work 21 sc across to opposite end of neck edge, turn. (*22 sc*)

Row 2: Ch 1, sc in each st across. Fasten off.

SHOE
MAKE 2.

Rnd 1: Ch 10, dc in 4th ch from hook (*first 3 chs count as first dc*), dc in each of next 5 chs, 5 dc in last ch, working on opposite side of ch, dc in each of next 5 chs, 2 dc in last ch, join in 3rd ch of beg ch-3. (*19 dc*)

Rnd 2: Ch 3, dc in same st, dc in each of next 6 sts, 2 dc in each of next 5 sts, dc in each of next 6 sts, 2 dc in last st, join in 3rd ch of beg ch-3. (*26 dc*)

Rnd 3: Ch 3, dc in each st around, join in 3rd ch of beg ch-3

Rnd 4: Ch 3, dc in each of next 8 sts, [dc dec in each of next 2 sts] 4 times, dc in each of last 9 sts, join in 3rd ch of beg ch-3. (*22 dc*)

Rnd 5: Ch 1, sc in each of first 9 sts, [sc dec in next 2 sts] twice, sc in each of last 9 sts, join in beg sc. Fasten off. (*20 sts*)

Sew 1 appliqué to toe.

PANTS

Rnd 1: Ch 60, sl st in first ch to form ring, ch 3, dc in each ch around, join in 3rd ch of beg ch-3. (*60 dc*)

Rnd 2: Ch 3, dc in each of next 4 sts, 2 dc in next st, [dc in each of next 5 sts, 2 dc in next st] around, join in 3rd ch of beg ch-3. (*70 dc*)

Rnds 3–4: Ch 3, dc in each st around, join in 3rd ch of beg ch-3.

Rnd 5: Ch 3, dc in each st around, join in 3rd ch of beg ch-3, ch 6, sk next 34 sts, sl st in next st, Fasten off.

LEGS
Rnd 1: Join in 4th ch of ch-6, ch 3, dc in next ch, dc dec in next ch and st, dc in each st across to one st before opposite side of ch-6, dc dec in next st and next ch, dc in each of last 2 chs, join in 3rd ch of beg ch-3. (*40 sts*)

Rnd 2: Ch 1, sc in each st around, join in beg sc. (*20 sc*)

Rnd 3: Ch 3, (dc, ch 2, 2 dc) in same st, sk next st, [shell in next st, sk next st] around, join in 3rd ch of beg ch-3. Fasten off. (*10 shells*)

Rnd 4: Ch 3, (dc, ch 2, 2 dc) in same st, sk next st, [shell in next st, sk next st] around, join in 3rd ch of beg ch-3. Fasten off. (*10 shells*)

Working on opposite side of ch-6, rep on other Leg opening.

Cut 2 lengths of ribbon, each 18 inches long, weave 1 strand ribbon through first rnd of sts on front and weave other strand ribbon through first rnd of sts on back.

Pull ribbon ends even, tie ends in bow at each side of Pants. ■

Little Star

THREAD
SKILL LEVEL

EASY

FINISHED SIZES
Instructions given fit small 8-inch chubby doll; changes for medium 10-inch cloth doll and large 12-inch cloth doll are in [ ].

FINISHED MEASUREMENTS
Chest: 8½ inches (*small*) [8½ inches (*medium*), 9 inches (*large*)]

MATERIALS
- Size 10 crochet cotton:
  350 yds cream
- Size steel crochet hook needed for size
  or size needed to obtain gauge
- Sewing needle
- ¼-inch buttons:
  2 white
- ¼-inch-wide cream ribbon:
  3 yds
- ¼-inch-wide ribbon roses with leaves:
  7 cream
- Cream sewing thread

GAUGE
Small & Medium Sizes: Size 7/1.65mm steel crochet hook: 15 dc = 2 inches; 8 dc rows = 2 inches

Large Size: Size 6/1.80mm steel crochet hook: 13 dc = 2 inches; 7 dc rows = 2 inches

PATTERN NOTES
Join with slip stitch as indicated unless otherwise stated.

Chain-3 at beginning of row or round counts as first double crochet unless otherwise stated.

Chain-6 at beginning of row or round counts as first double crochet and chain-3 space unless otherwise stated.

SPECIAL STITCHES
Shell: (2 dc, ch 2, 2 dc) in designated place.

Cluster (cl): (Sc, ch 2, 2 dc) in st or ch sp.

INSTRUCTIONS
DRESS
Row 1 (RS): Starting at neck, ch 41, sc in 2nd ch from hook and in each ch across, turn. (40 sc)

Row 2: Ch 3 (see Pattern Notes), dc in same st, dc in next st, [2 dc in next st, dc in next st] across, turn. (60 dc)

Row 3: Ch 3, dc in same st, dc in each of next 2 sts, [2 dc in next st, dc in each of next 2 sts] across, turn. (80 dc)

Row 4: Ch 3, dc in same st, dc in each of next 3 sts, [2 dc in next st, dc in each of next 3 sts] across, turn. (100 dc)

Row 5: Ch 3, dc in each of next 14 sts, for **armhole**, ch 5, sk next 20 sts, dc in each of next 30 sts, for **armhole**, ch 5, sk next 20 sts, dc in each of last 15 sts, turn. (60 dc, 10 chs)

Rnd 6: Now working in rnds, for **skirt**, ch 3, dc in each dc and ch around, **join** (see Pattern Notes) in 3rd ch of beg ch-3. (70 dc)

Rnd 7: Ch 6 (see Pattern Notes), [dc in each of next 7 sts, ch 3] around to last 6 sts, dc in each of last 6 sts, join in 3rd ch of beg ch-6. (10 7-dc groups, 10 ch-3 sps)

Rnd 8: Sl st in next ch after joining, sl st in ch-3 sp, ch 6, 2 dc in same ch-3 sp, [dc in each of next 3 sts, sk next st, dc in each of next 3 sts, shell in next ch sp] 9 times, dc in each of next 3 sts, sk next st, dc in each of last 3 dc, dc in beg ch-3 sp, join in 3rd ch of beg ch-6. (10 10-dc groups, 10 ch sps)

Rnds 9–24: Sl st in ch-3 sp, ch 6, 2 dc in same ch-3 sp, *dc in each st around to st directly before next sk st, sk next 2 sts**, dc in each st around to next shell, shell in ch-2 sp of next shell, rep from * around, ending last rep at **, dc in each st across to beg ch-3 sp, dc in beg ch-3 sp, join in 3rd ch of beg ch-6. Fasten off at end of last rnd.(20 21-dc groups, 10 ch sps)

SKIRT EDGING
Join with sc in ch-3 sp, (ch 2, 2 dc) in same sp, sk next st, *[cl in next st, sk next 2 sts] 6 times, sc in next st, [cl in next st, sk next 2 sts] 6 times, cl in next ch-3 sp, sk next 2 sts, rep from * 9 times, join in beg sc, fasten off.

NECK EDGING (OPTIONAL)
Working in starting ch on opposite side of row 1, join with sc in first ch, evenly sp 18 cls across to last ch, sc in last ch. Fasten off.

SLEEVES
Rnd 1: Join with sc around last dc before ch-5 on 1 armhole in row 5, hdc around same dc, working across 20 sk sts, dc in each of next 8 dc, 2 dc in next st, dc in each of next 2 sts, 2 dc in next st, dc in each of next 8 dc, hdc around

next dc in row 5, sc around same dc, working in opposite side of ch-5, sl st in each ch across, join in beg sc. *(31 sts)*

Rnd 2: Ch 1, sc in first st, hdc in next st, dc in each of next 22 sts, hdc in next st, sc in next st, sl st in each of next 5 sl sts, join in beg sc.

Rnd 3: Ch 1, sc in first st, hdc in next st, [**dc dec** *(see Stitch Guide)* in next 2 sts] 11 times, hdc in next st, sc in next st, sc in each of next 5 sts, join in beg sc. *(20 sts)*

Rnd 4: Ch 1, sc in each st around, join in beg sc. *(20 sc)*

Rnd 5: Ch 1, cl in first st, sk next st, [cl in next st, sk next st] around, join in beg sc. Fasten off.

Rep on other armhole.

Sew buttons 1 inch apart down left back opening using sps between sts on right back opening for buttonholes.

Cut 3 strands ribbon, each 15 inches long. Tie center of each ribbon strand into a 1-inch bow, leaving long ends for streamers.

Sew 3 bows evenly sp across front of bodice. Glue 1 ribbon rose to top of each bow *(see photo)*

BONNET
Rnd 1: Ch 6, join in beg ch to form ring, ch 3, dc in ring, ch 2, [2 dc in ring, ch 2] 5 times, join in 3rd ch of beg ch 3. *(12 dc, 6 ch sps)*

Rnds 2–4: Ch 3, dc in each st around with (dc, ch 2, dc) in each ch sp, join in 3rd ch of beg ch-3. Fasten off at end of last rnd. *(6 8-dc groups, 6 ch sps at end of last rnd)*

Row 5: Now working in rows, join in 6th st of any 8-dc group, ch 3, dc in each of next 2 sts, dc in next ch sp, ch 1, [dc in each of next 8 sts, dc in next ch sp, ch 1] 4 times, dc in each of next 4 sts, leaving rem sts and ch sps unworked, turn. *(44 dc, 5 ch-1 sps)*

Rows 6–12: Ch 3, dc in each of next 3 sts, [ch 1, dc in each of next 9 sts, 4 times, ch 1, dc in each of last 4 sts, turn.

Row 13: Ch 1, cl in first st, evenly sp 15 more cls across with sc in last st, **do not turn**.

Row 14: Ch 1, evenly sp 22 sc across lower neck edge of Bonnet, turn.

Row 15: Ch 1, sc in each st across. Fasten off.

For **ties**, weave 30 inches of ribbon through sts of row 11 from 1 side of Bonnet to other, pull ends even for ties.

BOW
MAKE 2.
Tie center of 18 inches of ribbon into a bow. Trim ends. Sew 1 ribbon rose to top of each bow.

Sew 1 bow to each side of Bonnet on each side of row 11 above ribbon ends.

SHOE
MAKE 2.
Rnd 1: Ch 10, dc in 4th ch from hook *(first 3 chs count as first dc)*, dc in each of next 5 chs, 5 dc in last ch, working on opposite side of ch, dc in each of next 5 chs, 2 dc in last ch, join in 3rd ch of beg ch-3. *(19 dc)*

Rnd 2: Ch 3, dc in same st, dc in each of next 6 sts, 2 dc in each of next 5 sts, dc in each of next 6 sts, 2 dc in last st, join in 3rd ch of beg ch-3. *(26 dc)*

Rnd 3: Ch 3, dc in each st around, join in 3rd ch of beg ch-3

Rnd 4: Ch 3, dc in each of next 8 sts, [dc dec in each of next 2 sts] 4 times, dc in each of last 9 sts, join in 3rd ch of beg ch-3. Fasten off. *(22 dc)*

Rnd 5: Ch 1, sc in each of first 9 sts, [sc dec in next 2 sts] twice, sc in each of last 9 sts, join in beg sc. Fasten off. *(20 sts)*

Make 2 bows the same as Bonnet Bows. Sew 1 to top of each Shoe.

PANTS
Rnd 1: Ch 60, sl st in first ch to form ring, ch 3, dc in each ch around, join in 3rd ch of beg ch-3. *(60 dc)*

Rnd 2: Ch 3, dc in each of next 4 sts, 2 dc in next st, [dc in each of next 5 sts, 2 dc in next st] around, join in 3rd ch of beg ch-3. *(70 dc)*

Rnds 3–4 [3–6, 3–9]: Ch 3, dc in each st around, join in 3rd ch of beg ch-3.

Rnd 5 [7, 10]: Ch 3, dc in each st around, join in 3rd ch of beg ch-3, ch 6, sk next 34 sts, sl st in next st. Fasten off.

LEGS
Rnd 1: Join in 4th ch of ch-6, ch 3, dc in next ch, dc dec in next ch and st, dc in each st across to one st before opposite side of ch-6, dc dec in next st and next ch, dc in each of last 2 chs, join in 3rd ch of beg ch 3. *(40 sts)*

Rnd 0 [2, 2]: Ch 3, dc in each st around, join in 3rd ch of beg ch-3.

Rnd 2 [3, 3]: Ch 1, **sc dec** *(see Stitch Guide)* in first 2 sts, [sc dec in next 2 sts] around, join in beg sc dec. *(20 sc dec)*

Rnd 3 [4, 4]: Ch 1, sc in each st around, join in beg sc.

Rnd 4 [5, 5]: Ch 1, cl in first st, sk next st, [cl in next st, sk next st] around, join in beg sc. Fasten off.

Working on opposite side of ch-6, rep on other Leg opening.

Cut 2 lengths of ribbon, each 18 inches long, weave 1 strand ribbon through first rnd of sts on front and weave other strand ribbon through first rnd of sts on back.

Pull ribbon ends even, tie ends in bow at each side of Pants.

YARN
SKILL LEVEL

EASY

FINISHED SIZE
Fits 10-inch chubby doll

FINISHED MEASUREMENT
Chest: 11 inches

MATERIALS
- Super fine (fingering) yarn: 2 oz/350 yds/57g cream
- Size C/2/2.75mm crochet hook or size needed to obtain gauge
- Sewing needle
- ³⁄₈-inch buttons: 2 white
- ¼-inch-wide cream ribbon: 3 yds
- ¼-inch-wide ribbon roses with leaves: 7 cream
- Cream sewing thread

GAUGE
5 dc = 1 inch; 5 dc rows = 1½ inches

PATTERN NOTES
Join with slip stitch as indicated unless otherwise stated.

Chain-3 at beginning of row or round counts as first double crochet unless otherwise stated.

Chain-6 at beginning of row or round counts as first double crochet and chain-3 space.

SPECIAL STITCHES
Shell: (2 dc, ch 2, 2 dc) in designated place.

Cluster (cl): (Sc, ch 2, 2 dc) in st or ch sp.

INSTRUCTIONS
DRESS
Row 1 (RS): Starting at neck, ch 41, sc in 2nd ch from hook and in each ch across, turn. *(40 sc)*

Row 2: Ch 3 *(see Pattern Notes)*, dc in same st, dc in next st, [2 dc in next st, dc in next st] across, turn. *(60 dc)*

Row 3: Ch 3, dc in same st, dc in each of next 2 sts, [2 dc in next st, dc in each of next 2 sts] across, turn. *(80 dc)*

Row 4: Ch 3, dc in same st, dc in each of next 3 sts, [2 dc in next st, dc in each of next 3 sts] across, turn. *(100 dc)*

Row 5: Ch 3, dc in each of next 14 sts, for **armhole**, ch 5, sk next 20 sts, dc in each of next 30 sts, for **armhole**, ch 5, sk next 20 sts, dc in each of last 15 sts, turn. *(60 dc, 10 chs)*

Rnd 6: Now working in rnds, for **skirt**, ch 3, dc in each dc and ch around, **join** *(see Pattern Notes)* in 3rd ch of beg ch-3. *(70 dc)*

Rnd 7: Ch 6 *(see Pattern Notes)*, [dc in each of next 7 sts, ch 3] around to last 6 sts, dc in each of last 6 sts, join in 3rd ch of beg ch-6. *(10 7-dc groups, 10 ch-3 sps)*

Rnd 8: Sl st in ch-3 sp, ch 6, 2 dc in same ch-3 sp, [dc in each of next 3 sts, sk next st, dc in each of next 3 sts, shell in next ch sp] 9 times, dc in each of next 3 sts, sk next st, join in 3rd ch of beg ch-6. *(10 10-dc groups, 10 ch sps)*

Rnds 9–24: Sl st in ch-3 sp, ch 6, 2 dc in same ch-3 sp, *dc in each st around to st directly before next sk st, sk next 2 sts**, dc in each st around to next shell, shell in ch-2 sp of next shell, rep from * around, ending last rep at **, dc in each st across to beg ch-3 sp, dc in beg ch-3 sp, join in 3rd ch of beg ch-6. Fasten off at end of last rnd.*(20 21-dc groups, 10 ch sps)*

SKIRT EDGING
Join with sc in ch-3 sp, (ch 2, 2 dc) in same sp, sk next st, [cl in next st, sk next st] 6 times, sc in next st, *[cl in next st, sk next st] 13 times, sc in next st, rep from * 9 times, cl in next st, sk next st] 6 times, join in beg sc. Fasten off.

NECK EDGING (OPTIONAL)
Working in starting ch on opposite side of row 1, join with sc in first ch, evenly sp 18 cls across to last ch, sc in last ch. Fasten off.

SLEEVES
Rnd 1: Join with sc around last dc before ch-5 on 1 armhole in row 5, hdc around same dc, working across 20 sk sts, dc in each of next 8 dc, 2 dc in next st, dc in each of next 2 sts, 2 dc in next st, dc in each of next 8 dc, hdc around next dc in row 5, sc around same dc, working in opposite side of ch-5, sl st in each ch across, join in beg sc. *(31 sts)*

Rnd 2: Ch 1, sc in first st, hdc in next st, dc in each of next 22 sts, hdc in next st, sc in next st, sl st in each of next 5 sl sts, join in beg sc.

Rnd 3: Ch 1, sc in first st, hdc in next st, [**dc dec** *(see Stitch Guide)* in next 2 sts] 11 times, hdc in next st, sc in next st, sc in each of next 5 sts, join in beg sc.

Rnd 4: Ch 1, sc in each st around, join in beg sc. *(20 sc)*

Rnd 5: Ch 1, cl in first st, sk next st, [cl in next st, sk next st] around, join in beg sc. Fasten off.

Rep on other armhole.

Sew buttons 1 inch apart down left back opening using sps between sts on right back opening for buttonholes.

Cut 3 strands ribbon, each 15 inches long. Tie center of each ribbon strand into a 1-inch bow, leaving long ends for streamers.

Sew 3 bows evenly sp across front of bodice. Glue 1 ribbon rose to top of each bow. *(see photo)*

BONNET
Rnd 1: Ch 6, join in beg ch to form ring, ch 3, dc in ring, ch 2, [2 dc in ring, ch 2] 5 times, join in 3rd ch of beg ch 3. *(12 dc, 6 ch sps)*

Rnds 2–4: Ch 3, dc in each st around with (dc, ch 2, dc) in each ch sp, join in 3rd ch of beg ch-3. Fasten off at end of last rnd. *(6 8-dc groups, 6 ch sps at end of last rnd)*

Row 5: Now working in rows, join in 6th st of any 8-dc group, ch 3, dc in each of next 2 sts, dc in next ch sp, ch 1, [dc in each of next 8 sts, dc in next ch sp, ch 1] 4 times, dc in each of next 4 sts, leaving rem sts and ch sps unworked, turn. *(44 dc, 5 ch-1 sps)*

Rows 6–12: Ch 3, dc in each of next 3 sts, [ch 1, dc in each of next 9 sts] 4 times, ch 1, dc in each of last 4 sts, turn.

Row 13: Ch 1, cl in first st, evenly sp 15 more cls across with sc in last st, **do not turn.**

Row 14: Ch 1, evenly sp 22 sc across lower neck edge of Bonnet, turn.

Row 15: Ch 1, sc in each st across. Fasten off.

For **ties,** weave 30 inches of ribbon through sts of rnd 11 from 1 side of Bonnet to other, pull ends even for ties.

BOW
MAKE 2.
Tie center of 18 inches of ribbon into a bow. Trim ends. Sew 1 ribbon rose to top of each bow.

Sew 1 bow to each side of Bonnet on row 11 above ends.

SHOE
MAKE 2.
Rnd 1: Ch 10, dc in 4th ch from hook *(first 3 chs count as first dc)*, dc in each of next 5 chs, 5 dc in last ch, working on opposite side of ch, dc in each of next 5 chs, 2 dc in last ch, join in 3rd ch of beg ch-3. *(19 dc)*

Rnd 2: Ch 3, dc in same st, dc in each of next 6 sts, 2 dc in each of next 5 sts, dc in each of next 6 sts, 2 dc in last st, join in 3rd ch of beg ch-3. *(26 dc)*

Rnd 3: Ch 3, dc in each st around, join in 3rd ch of beg ch-3

Rnd 4: Ch 3, dc in each of next 8 sts, [dc dec in each of next 2 sts] 4 times, dc in each of last 9 sts, join in 3rd ch of beg ch-3. Fasten off. *(22 dc)*

Rnd 5: Ch 1, sc in each of first 9 sts, [sc dec in next 2 sts] twice, sc in each of last 9 sts, join in beg sc. Fasten off. *(20 sts)*

Make 2 bows same as Bonnet Bows. Sew 1 to top of each Shoe.

PANTS
Rnd 1: Ch 60, sl st in first ch to form ring, ch 3, dc in each ch around, join in 3rd ch of beg ch-3. *(60 dc)*

Rnd 2: Ch 3, dc in each of next 4 sts, 2 dc in next st, [dc in each of next 5 sts, 2 dc in next st] around, join in 3rd ch of beg ch-3. *(70 dc)*

Rnds 3 & 4: Ch 3, dc in each st around, join in 3rd ch of beg ch-3.

Rnd 5: Ch 3, dc in each st around, join in 3rd ch of ch-3, ch 6, sk next 34 sts, sl st in next st. Fasten off.

LEGS
Rnd 1: Join in 4th ch of ch-6, ch 3, dc in next ch, dc dec in next ch and st, dc in each st across to one st before opposite side of ch-6, dc dec in next st and next ch, dc in each of last 2 chs, join in 3rd ch of beg ch-3. *(40 sts)*

Rnd 2: Ch 1, **sc dec** *(see Stitch Guide)* in first 2 sts, [sc dec in next 2 sts] around, join in beg sc dec. *(20 sc dec)*

Rnd 3: Ch 1, sc in each st around, join in beg sc. *(20 sc)*

Rnd 4: Ch 3, 2 dc in same st, sk next st, [cl in next st, sk next st] around, join in 1st ch of beg ch-3. Fasten off. *(10 cl)*

Working on opposite side of ch-6, rep on other Leg opening.

Cut 2 lengths of ribbon, each 18 inches long, weave 1 strand ribbon through first rnd of sts on front and weave other strand ribbon through first rnd of sts on back.

Pull ribbon ends even, tie ends in bow at each side of Pants.∎

Nautical

THREAD
SKILL LEVEL

EASY

FINISHED SIZES

Instructions given fit small 8-inch chubby doll; changes for medium 10-inch cloth doll and large 12-inch cloth doll are in [ ].

FINISHED MEASUREMENTS

Chest: 8½ inches *(small)* [8½ inches *(medium)*, 9 inches *(large)*]

MATERIALS

- Size 10 crochet cotton:
    350 yds blue
    10 yds white
- Size steel crochet hook needed for size or size needed to obtain gauge
- Sewing needle
- Buttons:
    ½-inch: red star
    ¼-inch: 2 white
- Sailboat appliqué
- White and red sewing thread

GAUGE

Small & Medium Sizes: Size 7/1.65mm steel crochet hook: 15 dc = 2 inches; 8 dc rows = 2 inches

Large Size: Size 6/1.80mm steel crochet hook: 13 dc = 2 inches; 7 dc rows = 2 inches

PATTERN NOTES

Join with slip stitch as indicated unless otherwise stated.

Chain-3 at beginning of row or round counts as first double crochet unless otherwise stated.

SPECIAL STITCH

Shell: (2 dc, ch 2, sc) in next st or ch.

INSTRUCTIONS
ROMPER

Row 1 (RS): Starting at neck, with blue, ch 41, sc in 2nd ch from hook and in each ch across, turn. *(40 sc)*

Row 2: Ch 3 *(see Pattern Notes)*, dc in each of next 5 sts, (2 dc, ch 2, 2 dc) in next st, dc in each of next 6 sts, (2 dc, ch 2, 2 dc) in next st, dc in each of next 12 sts, (2 dc, ch 2, 2 dc) in next st, dc in each of next 6 sts, (2 dc, ch 2, 2 dc) in next st, dc in each of last 6 sts, turn. *(52 sts, 4 ch-2 sps)*

Row 3: Ch 3, dc in each of next 7 sts, (2 dc, ch 2, 2 dc) in next ch-2 sp, dc in each of next 10 sts, (2 dc, ch 2, 2 dc) in next ch-2 sp, dc in each of next 16 sts, (2 dc, ch 2, 2 dc) in next ch-2 sp, dc in each of next 10 sts, (2 dc, ch 2, 2 dc) in next ch-2 sp, dc in each of next 8 sts, turn. *(68 dc, 4 ch sps)*

Row 4: Ch 3, dc in each of next 9 sts, (2 dc, ch 2, 2 dc) in next ch-2 sp, dc in each of next 14 sts, (2 dc, ch 2, 2 dc) in next ch-2 sp, dc in each of next 20 sts, (2 dc, ch 2, 2 dc) in next ch-2 sp, dc in each of next 14 sts, (2 dc, ch 2, 2 dc) in next ch-2 sp, dc in each of last 10 sts, turn. *(84 dc)*

Row 5: Ch 3, dc in each of next 11 sts, (2 dc, ch 2, 2 dc) in next ch-2 sp, dc in each of next 18 sts, (2 dc, ch 2, 2 dc) in next ch-2 sp, dc in each of next 24 sts, (2 dc, ch 2, 2 dc) in next ch-2 sp, dc in each of next 18 sts, (2 dc, ch 2, 2 dc) in next ch-2 sp, dc in each of last 12 sts, turn. *(100 dc)*

Row 6: Ch 1, sc in each of first 14 sts, sc in next ch sp, for **armhole**, ch 5, sk next 22 sts, sc in next ch sp, sc in each of next 28 sts, sc in next ch sp, for **armhole**, ch 5, sk next 22 sts, sc in next ch-2 sp, sc in each of last 14 sts, turn. *(70 sts and chs)*

Row 7: Ch 3, (dc, ch 2, sc) in same st, [sk next 2 sts or chs, **shell** *(see Special Stitch)* in next st or ch] across, turn. *(24 shells)*

Row 8: Ch 3 (dc, ch 2, sc) in first st, shell in each ch-2 sp across, turn.

Rep row 8 until desired length or 4¼ [4¼, 5½] inches from beg. At end of last row, **join** *(see Pattern Notes)* in 3rd ch of beg ch-3. **Do not turn** at end of last row.

LEG BANDS
Row 1: Ch 7, sc in last sc of 12th shell. Fasten off.

Rnd 2: Now working in rnds around 1 leg opening, join blue in 4th ch of ch-7, ch 2 *(counts as first hdc)*, evenly sp 30 more hdc around opening, join in 2nd ch of beg ch-2. *(31 hdc)*

Rnds 3 & 4: Ch 2, hdc in each st around, join in 2nd ch of beg ch-2. Fasten off at end of last rnd.

Rnd 5: For **trim**, working in **back lps** *(see Stitch Guide)*, join white with sc in first st, sc in each st around,

Working on opposite side of ch-7, rep rnds 2–5 on other leg opening.

SLEEVES
Rnd 1: Working around 1 armhole, join blue with sc at bottom center of armhole, evenly sp 30 sc around armhole, join in beg sc. *(31 sc)*

Rnd 2: Ch 1, sc in each st around, join in beg sc. Fasten off.

Rnd 3: Working this rnd in back lps, join white with sc in first st, sc in each st around, join in beg sc. Fasten off.

Rep on other armhole opening.

NECK TRIM
Working in starting ch on opposite side of row 1, join white with sc in first ch, sc in each ch across with sc dec in next 3 sts in each corner. Fasten off.

Sew white buttons evenly sp to left back opening using sp between sts on right back for buttonholes.

Sew sailboat appliqué to center front.

BERET
Rnd 1: With blue, ch 5, join in beg ch to form ring, ch 3, 11 dc in ring, join in 3rd ch of beg ch-3. *(12 dc)*

Rnd 2: Ch 3, dc in same st, 2 dc in each st around, join in 3rd ch of beg ch-3. *(24 dc)*

Rnd 3: Ch 3, 2 dc in next st, [dc in next st, 2 dc in next st] around, join in 3rd ch of beg ch-3. *(36 dc)*

Rnd 4: Ch 3, dc in next st, 2 dc in next st, [dc in each of next 2 sts, 2 dc in next st] around, join in 3rd ch of beg ch-3. *(48 dc)*

Rnd 5: Ch 3, dc in each of next 2 sts, 2 dc in next st, [dc in each of next 3 sts, 2 dc in next st] around, join in 3rd ch of beg ch-3. *(60 dc)*

Rnd 6: Ch 3, dc in each of next 3 sts, 2 dc in next st, [dc in each of next 4 sts, 2 dc in next st] around, join in 3rd ch of beg ch-3. *(72 dc)*

Rnds 7 & 8: Ch 3, dc in each st around, join in 3rd ch of beg ch-3.

Rnd 9: Ch 3, dc in each of next 2 sts, **dc dec** *(see Stitch Guide)* in next 2 sts, [dc in each of next 4 sts, dc dec in next 2 sts] around, join in 3rd ch of beg ch-3. *(60 dc)*

Rnd 10: Ch 3, dc in each of next 2 sts, dc dec in next 2 sts, [dc in each of next 3 sts, dc dec in next 2 sts] around, join in 3rd ch of beg ch-3. *(48 dc)*

Rnds 11 & 12: Ch 2 *(counts as first hdc)*, hdc in each st around, join in 2nd ch of beg ch-2. Fasten off at end of last rnd.

Rnd 13: Working this rnd in back lps, join white with sc in first st, sc in each st around, join in beg sc. Fasten off.

CROCHET BUTTON

With white, ch 2, 12 sc in 2nd ch from hook, join in beg sc. Fasten off.

Sew Crochet Button to top of Beret.

Sew star button to side of Beret close to last rnd.

BOOTIE
MAKE 2.

Rnd 1: With blue, ch 10, dc in 4th ch from hook *(first 3 chs count as first dc)*, dc in each of next 5 chs, 5 dc in last ch, working on opposite side of ch, dc in each of next 5 chs, 2 dc in last ch, join in 3rd ch of beg ch-3. *(19 dc)*

Rnd 2: Ch 3, dc in same st, dc in each of next 6 sts, 2 dc in each of next 5 sts, dc in each of next 6 sts, 2 dc in last st, join in 3rd ch of beg ch-3. *(26 dc)*

Rnd 3: Ch 3, dc in each st around, join in 3rd ch of beg ch-3.

Rnd 4: Ch 3, dc in each of next 8 sts, [dc dec in next 2 sts] 4 times, dc in each of last 9 sts, join in 3rd ch of beg ch-3. *(22 sts)*

Rnd 5: Ch 1, sc in each of first 7 sts, hdc in each of next 2 sts, [dc dec in next 2 sts] twice, hdc in each of next 2 sts, sc in each of last 7 sts, join in beg sc. (20 sts)

Rnds 6 & 7: Ch 3, dc in each st around, join in 3rd ch of beg ch-3. Fasten off at end of last rnd.

Rnd 8: Working this rnd in back lps, join white with sc in first st, sc in each st around, join in beg sc. Fasten off.

TIE

With white, ch for 12 inches. Fasten off.

Weave Tie through sts of rnd 6, tie ends into a bow at center front.

YARN
SKILL LEVEL

EASY

FINISHED SIZE

Fits 10-inch chubby doll

FINISHED MEASUREMENT

Chest: 11 inches

MATERIALS

- Super fine (fingering) yarn:
  2 oz/350 yds/57g blue
  20 yds white
- Sizes C/2/2.75mm and D/3/3.25mm crochet hooks or size needed to obtain gauge
- Sewing needle
- Buttons:
  ¾-inch: red star
  ⅜-inch: 2 white
- Sailboat appliqué
- White sewing thread

1 SUPER FINE

GAUGE
Size C hook: 6 dc = 1 inch; 5 dc rows = 1½ inches

Size D hook: 5 dc = 1 inch; 4 dc rows = 1½ inches

PATTERN NOTES
Join with slip stitch as indicated unless otherwise stated.

Chain-3 at beginning of row or round counts as first double crochet unless otherwise stated.

SPECIAL STITCH
Shell: (2 dc, ch 2, sc) in next st or ch.

INSTRUCTIONS
ROMPER
Row 1 (RS): Starting at neck, with size C hook and blue, ch 41, sc in 2nd ch from hook and in each ch across, turn. *(40 sc)*

Row 2: Ch 3 *(see Pattern Notes)*, dc in each of next 5 sts, (2 dc, ch 2, 2 dc) in next st, dc in each of next 6 sts, (2 dc, ch 2, 2 dc) in next st, dc in each of next 12 sts, (2 dc, ch 2, 2 dc) in next st, dc in each of next 6 sts, (2 dc, ch 2, 2 dc) in next st, dc in each of last 6 sts, turn. *(52 sts, 4 ch-2 sps)*

Row 3: Ch 3, dc in each of next 7 sts, (2 dc, ch 2, 2 dc) in next ch-2 sp, dc in each of next 10 sts, (2 dc, ch 2, 2 dc) in next ch-2 sp, dc in each of next 16 sts, (2 dc, ch 2, 2 dc) in next ch-2 sp, dc in each of next 10 sts, (2 dc, ch 2, 2 dc) in next ch-2 sp, dc in each of next 8 sts, turn. *(68 dc, 4 ch sps)*

Row 4: Ch 3, dc in each of next 9 sts, (2 dc, ch 2, 2 dc) in next ch-2 sp, dc in each of next 14 sts, (2 dc, ch 2, 2 dc) in next ch-2 sp, dc in each of next 20 sts, (2 dc, ch 2, 2 dc) in next ch-2 sp, dc in each of next 14 sts, (2 dc, ch 2, 2 dc) in next ch-2 sp, dc in each of last 10 sts, turn. *(84 dc)*

Row 5: Ch 3, dc in each of next 11 sts, (2 dc, ch 2, 2 dc) in next ch-2 sp, dc in each of next 18 sts, (2 dc, ch 2, 2 dc) in next ch-2 sp, dc in each of next 24 sts, (2 dc, ch 2, 2 dc) in next ch-2 sp, dc in each of next 18 sts, (2 dc, ch 2, 2 dc) in next ch-2 sp, dc in each of last 12 sts, turn. *(100 dc)*

Row 6: Ch 1, sc in each of first 14 sts, sc in next ch sp, for **armhole**, ch 5, sk next 22 sts, sc in next ch sp, sc in each of next 28 sts, sc in next ch sp, for **armhole**, ch 5, sk next 22 sts, sc in next ch-2 sp, sc in each of last 14 sts, turn. *(70 sts and chs)*

Row 7: Ch 3, (dc, ch 2, sc) in same st, [sk next 2 sts or chs, **shell** *(see Special Stitch)* in next st or ch] across, turn. *(24 shells)*

Row 8: Ch 3 (dc, ch 2, sc) in first st, shell in each ch-2 sp across, turn.

Rep row 8 until desired length or 5 inches from beg. At end of last row, **join** *(see Pattern Notes)* in 3rd ch of beg ch-3. **Do not turn** at end of last row.

LEG BANDS
Row 1: Ch 7, sc in last sc of 12th shell. Fasten off.

Rnd 2: Now working in rnds around 1 leg opening, join blue in 4th ch of ch-7, ch 2 *(counts as first hdc)*, evenly sp 30 more hdc around opening, join in 2nd ch of beg ch-2. *(31 hdc)*

Rnds 3 & 4: Ch 2, hdc in each st around, join in 2nd ch of beg ch-2. Fasten off at end of last rnd.

Rnd 5: For **trim**, working in **back lps** *(see Stitch Guide)* join white with sc in first st, sc in each st around,

Working on opposite side of ch-7, rep rnds 2–5 on other leg opening.

SLEEVES
Rnd 1: Working around 1 armhole, join blue with sc at bottom center of armhole, evenly sp 30 sc around armhole, join in beg sc. *(31 sc)*

Rnd 2: Ch 1, sc in each st around, join in beg sc. Fasten off.

Rnd 3: Working this rnd in back lps, join white with sc in first st, sc in each st around, join in beg sc. Fasten off.

Rep on other armhole opening.

NECK TRIM

Working in starting ch on opposite side of row 1, join white with sc in first ch, sc in each ch across with sc dec in next 3 sts in each corner. Fasten off.

Sew white buttons evenly sp to left back opening using sp between sts on right back for buttonholes.

Sew sailboat appliqué to center front.

BERET

Rnd 1: With size D hook and blue, ch 5, join in beg ch to form ring, ch 3, 11 dc in ring, join in 3rd ch of beg ch-3. *(12 dc)*

Rnd 2: Ch 3, dc in same st, 2 dc in each st around, join in 3rd ch of beg ch-3. *(24 dc)*

Rnd 3: Ch 3, 2 dc in next st, [dc in next st, 2 dc in next st] around, join in 3rd ch of beg ch-3. *(36 dc)*

Rnd 4: Ch 3, dc in next st, 2 dc in next st, [dc in each of next 2 sts, 2 dc in next st] around, join in 3rd ch of beg ch-3. *(48 dc)*

Rnd 5: Ch 3, dc in each of next 2 sts, 2 dc in next st, [dc in each of next 3 sts, 2 dc in next st] around, join in 3rd ch of beg ch-3. *(60 dc)*

Rnd 6: Ch 3, dc in each of next 3 sts, 2 dc in next st, [dc in each of next 4 sts, 2 dc in next st] around, join in 3rd ch of beg ch-3. *(72 dc)*

Rnds 7 & 8: Ch 3, dc in each st around, join in 3rd ch of beg ch-3.

Rnd 9: Ch 3, dc in each of next 2 sts, **dc dec** (*see Stitch Guide*) in next 2 sts, [dc in each of next 4 sts, dc dec in next 2 sts] around, join in 3rd ch of beg ch-3. *(60 dc)*

Rnd 10: Ch 3, dc in each of next 2 sts, dc dec in next 2 sts, [dc in each of next 3 sts, dc dec in next 2 sts] around, join in 3rd ch of beg ch-3. *(48 dc)*

Rnds 11 & 12: Ch 2 *(counts as first hdc)*, hdc in each st around, join in 2nd ch of beg ch-2. Fasten off at end of last rnd.

Rnd 13: Working this rnd in back lps, join white with sc in first st, sc in each st around, join in beg sc. Fasten off.

CROCHET BUTTON

With white, ch 2, 12 sc in 2nd ch from hook, join in beg sc. Fasten off.

Sew Crochet Button to top of Beret.

Sew star button to side of Beret close to last rnd.

BOOTIE
MAKE 2.

Rnd 1: With size C hook and blue, ch 10, dc in 4th ch from hook (*first 3 chs count as first dc*), dc in each of next 5 chs, 5 dc in last ch, working on opposite side of ch, dc in each of next 5 chs, 2 dc in last ch, join in 3rd ch of beg ch-3. *(19 dc)*

Rnd 2: Ch 3, dc in same st, dc in each of next 6 sts, 2 dc in each of next 5 sts, dc in each of next 6 sts, 2 dc in last st, join in 3rd ch of beg ch-3. *(26 dc)*

Rnd 3: Ch 3, dc in each st around, join in 3rd ch of beg ch-3.

Rnd 4: Ch 3, dc in each of next 8 sts, [dc dec in next 2 sts] 4 times, dc in each of last 9 sts, join in 3rd ch of beg ch-3. *(22 sts)*

Rnd 5: Ch 1, sc in each of first 7 sts, hdc in each of next 2 sts, [dc dec in next 2 sts] twice, hdc in each of next 2 sts, sc in each of last 7 sts, join in beg sc. *(20 sts)*

Rnds 6 & 7: Ch 3, dc in each st around, join in 3rd ch of beg ch-3. Fasten off at end of last rnd.

Rnd 8: Working this rnd in back lps, join white with sc in first st, sc in each st around, join in beg sc. Fasten off.

TIE

With blue, ch for 12 inches. Fasten off.

Weave Tie through sts of rnd 6, tie ends into a bow at center front.■

Sweet Plum

THREAD SKILL LEVEL

EASY

FINISHED SIZES

Instructions given fit small 8-inch chubby doll; changes for medium 10-inch cloth doll and large 12-inch cloth doll are in [ ].

FINISHED MEASUREMENTS

Chest: 8½ inches *(small)* [8½ inches *(medium)*, 9 inches *(large)*]

MATERIALS

- Size 10 crochet cotton:
  350 yds variegated plum
  50 yds white
- Size steel crochet hook needed for size or size needed to obtain gauge
- Sewing needle
- ¼-inch buttons:
  2 white
- Millinery flowers:
  ¾-inch-wide: 2 purple
  ½-inch-wide: 2 pink
- White sewing thread

GAUGE

Small & Medium Sizes: Size 7/1.65mm steel crochet hook: 15 dc = 2 inches; 8 dc rows = 2 inches

Large Size: Size 6/1.80mm steel crochet hook: 13 dc = 2 inches; 7 dc rows = 2 inches

PATTERN NOTES

Join with slip stitch as indicated unless otherwise stated.

Chain-3 at beginning of row or round counts as first double crochet unless otherwise stated.

SPECIAL STITCH

Shell: (2 dc, ch 2, sc) in next st or ch.

INSTRUCTIONS
ROMPER

Row 1 (RS): Starting at neck with white, ch 41, sc in 2nd ch from hook and in each ch across, turn. *(40 sc)*

Row 2: Ch 3 *(see Pattern Notes)*, dc in each of next 5 sts, (2 dc, ch 2, 2 dc) in next st, dc in each of next 6 sts, (2 dc, ch 2, 2 dc) in next st, dc in each of next 12 sts, (2 dc, ch 2, 2 dc) in next st, dc in each of next 6 sts, (2 dc, ch 2, 2 dc) in next st, dc in each of last 6 sts, turn. *(52 sts, 4 ch-2 sps)*

Row 3: Ch 3, dc in each of next 7 sts, (2 dc, ch 2, 2 dc) in next ch-2 sp, dc in each of next 10 sts, (2 dc, ch 2, 2 dc) in next ch-2 sp, dc in each of next 16 sts, (2 dc, ch 2, 2 dc) in next ch-2 sp, dc in each of next 10 sts, (2 dc, ch 2, 2 dc) in next ch-2 sp, dc in each of next 8 sts, turn. *(68 dc, 4 ch sps)*

Row 4: Ch 3, dc in each of next 9 sts, (2 dc, ch 2, 2 dc) in next ch-2 sp, dc in each of next 14 sts, (2 dc, ch 2, 2 dc) in next ch-2 sp, dc in each of next 20 sts, (2 dc, ch 2, 2 dc) in next ch-2 sp, dc in each of next 14 sts, (2 dc, ch 2, 2 dc) in next ch-2 sp, dc in each of last 10 sts, turn. *(84 dc)*

Row 5: Ch 3, dc in each of next 11 sts, (2 dc, ch 2, 2 dc) in next ch-2 sp, dc in each of next 18 sts, (2 dc, ch 2, 2 dc) in next ch-2 sp, dc in each of next 24 sts, (2 dc, ch 2, 2 dc) in next ch-2 sp, dc in each of next 18 sts, (2 dc, ch 2, 2 dc) in next ch-2 sp, dc in each of last 12 sts, turn. *(100 dc)*

Row 6: Ch 1, sc in each of first 14 sts, sc in next ch sp, for **armhole**, ch 5, sk next 22 sts, sc in next ch sp, sc in each of next 28 sts, sc in next ch sp, for **armhole**, ch 5, sk next 22 sts, sc in next ch-2 sp, sc in each of last 14 sts, turn. Fasten off. *(70 sts and chs)*

Row 7: Join *(see Pattern Notes)* with variegated plum in first st, ch 3, (dc, ch 2, sc) in same st, [sk next 2 sts or chs, **shell** *(see Special Stitch)* in next st or ch] across, turn. *(24 shells)*

Row 8: Ch 3 (dc, ch 2, sc) in first st, shell in each ch-2 sp across, turn.

Rep row 8 until desired length or 4¼ [4¼, 5½] inches from beg. At end of last row, **join** *(see Pattern Notes)* in 3rd ch of beg ch-3. **Do not turn** at end of last row.

LEG BANDS
Row 1: Ch 7, sc in last sc of 12th shell. Fasten off.

Rnd 2: Now working in rnds around 1 leg opening, join white in 4th ch of ch-7, ch 2 *(counts as first hdc)*, evenly sp 30 more hdc around opening, join in 2nd ch of beg ch-2. *(31 hdc)*

Rnds 3 & 4: Ch 2, hdc in each st around, join in 2nd ch of beg ch-2. Fasten off at end of last row.

Working on opposite side of ch-7, rep rnds 2–4 on other leg opening.

SLEEVES
Rnd 1: Working around 1 armhole, join white with sc at bottom center of armhole, evenly sp 30 sc around armhole, join in beg sc. *(31 sc)*

Rnd 2: Ch 1, sc in each st around, join in beg sc. Fasten off.

Rep on other armhole opening.

Sew white buttons evenly sp to left back opening using sp between sts on right back for buttonholes.

Sew 1 purple flower to center front at lower edge of white section *(see photo)*. Sew 1 pink flower to each side of purple flower

NECK TRIM
Working in starting ch on opposite side of row 1, join variegated plum with sc in first ch, sc in each ch across with sc dec in next 3 sts in each corner. Fasten off.

BERET
Rnd 1: With variegated plum, ch 5, join in beg ch to form ring, ch 3, 11 dc in ring, join in 3rd ch of beg ch-3. *(12 dc)*

Rnd 2: Ch 3, dc in same st, 2 dc in each st around, join in 3rd ch of beg ch-3. *(24 dc)*

Rnd 3: Ch 3, 2 dc in next st, [dc in next st, 2 dc in next st] around, join in 3rd ch of beg ch-3. *(36 dc)*

Rnd 4: Ch 3, dc in next st, 2 dc in next st, [dc in each of next 2 sts, 2 dc in next st] around, join in 3rd ch of beg ch-3. *(48 dc)*

Rnd 5: Ch 3, dc in each of next 2 sts, 2 dc in next st, [dc in each of next 3 sts, 2 dc in next st] around, join in 3rd ch of beg ch-3. *(60 dc)*

Rnd 6: Ch 3, dc in each of next 3 sts, 2 dc in next st, [dc in each of next 4 sts, 2 dc in next st] around, join in 3rd ch of beg ch-3. *(72 dc)*

Rnds 7 & 8: Ch 3, dc in each st around, join in 3rd ch of beg ch-3.

Rnd 9: Ch 3, dc in each of next 2 sts, **dc dec** *(see Stitch Guide)* in next 2 sts, [dc in each of next 4 sts, dc dec in next 2 sts] around, join in 3rd ch of beg ch-3. *(60 dc)*

Rnd 10: Ch 3, dc in each of next 2 sts, dc dec in next 2 sts, [dc in each of next 3 sts, dc dec in next 2 sts] around, join in 3rd ch of beg ch-3. Fasten off. *(48 dc)*

Rnd 11: Join white in first st, ch 2 *(counts as first hdc)*, hdc in each st around, join in 2nd ch of beg ch-2.

Rnds 12 & 13: Ch 2, hdc in each st around, join in 2nd ch of beg ch-2. Fasten off at end of last rnd.

CROCHET BUTTON

With white, ch 2, 12 sc in 2nd ch from hook, join in beg sc. Fasten off.

Sew Crochet Button to top of Beret.

Sew other purple flower to side of Beret close to last rnd.

BOOTIE
MAKE 2.
Rnd 1: With white, ch 10, dc in 4th ch from hook *(first 3 chs count as first dc)*, dc in each of next 5 chs, 5 dc in last ch, working on opposite side of ch, dc in each of next 5 chs, 2 dc in last ch, join in 3rd ch of beg ch-3. *(19 dc)*

Rnd 2: Ch 3, dc in same st, dc in each of next 6 sts, 2 dc in each of next 5 sts, dc in each of next 6 sts, 2 dc in last st, join in 3rd ch of beg ch-3. *(26 dc)*

Rnd 3: Ch 3, dc in each st around, join in 3rd ch of beg ch-3.

Rnd 4: Ch 3, dc in each of next 8 sts, [dc dec in next 2 sts] 4 times, dc in each of last 9 sts, join in 3rd ch of beg ch-3. *(22 sts)*

Rnd 5: Ch 1, sc in each of first 7 sts, hdc in each of next 2 sts, [dc dec in next 2 sts] twice, hdc in each of next 2 sts, sc in each of last 7 sts, join in beg sc. *(20 sts)*

Rnds 6 & 7: Ch 3, dc in each st around, join in 3rd ch of beg ch-3. Fasten off at end of last rnd.

Rnd 8: Working this rnd in back lps, join variegated plum with sc in first st, sc in each st around, join in beg sc. Fasten off.

TIE
With variegated plum, ch for 12 inches. Fasten off.

Weave Tie through sts of rnd 6, tie ends into a bow at center front.■

YARN
SKILL LEVEL

EASY

FINISHED SIZE
Fits 10-inch chubby doll

FINISHED MEASUREMENT
Chest: 11 inches

MATERIALS

- Super fine (fingering) yarn:
  2 oz/350 yds/57g variegated plum
  50 yds white
- Sizes C/2/2.75mm and D/3/3.25mm crochet
  hooks or sizes needed to obtain gauge
- Sewing needle
- ⅜-inch buttons:
  2 white
- Millinery flowers:
  ¾-inch wide: 2 dark purple
  ½-inch wide: 2 light purple
- White sewing thread

GAUGE

Size C hook: 6 dc = 1 inch; 5 dc rows = 1½ inches

Size D hook: 5 dc = 1 inch; 4 dc rows = 1½ inches

PATTERN NOTES

Join with slip stitch as indicated unless
otherwise stated.

Chain-3 at beginning of row or round counts as
first double crochet unless otherwise stated.

SPECIAL STITCH

Shell: (2 dc, ch 2, sc) in next st or ch.

INSTRUCTIONS
ROMPER

Row 1 (RS): Starting at neck, with size C hook
and white, ch 41, sc in 2nd ch from hook and in
each ch across, turn. (40 sc)

Row 2: Ch 3 (see Pattern Notes), dc in each of
next 5 sts, (2 dc, ch 2, 2 dc) in next st, dc in
each of next 6 sts, (2 dc, ch 2, 2 dc) in next st,
dc in each of next 12 sts, (2 dc, ch 2, 2 dc) in
next st, dc in each of next 6 sts, (2 dc, ch 2, 2
dc) in next st, dc in each of last 6 sts, turn.
(52 sts, 4 ch-2 sps)

Row 3: Ch 3, dc in each of next 7 sts, (2 dc, ch 2,
2 dc) in next ch-2 sp, dc in each of next 10 sts,
(2 dc, ch 2, 2 dc) in next ch-2 sp, dc in each of
next 16 sts, (2 dc, ch 2, 2 dc) in next ch-2 sp,
dc in each of next 10 sts, (2 dc, ch 2, 2 dc) in
next ch-2 sp, dc in each of next 8 sts, turn.
(68 dc, 4 ch sps)

Row 4: Ch 3, dc in each of next 9 sts, (2 dc, ch 2,
2 dc) in next ch-2 sp, dc in each of next 14 sts,
(2 dc, ch 2, 2 dc) in next ch-2 sp, dc in each of
next 20 sts, (2 dc, ch 2, 2 dc) in next ch-2 sp, dc
in each of next 14 sts, (2 dc, ch 2, 2 dc) in next
ch-2 sp, dc in each of last 10 sts, turn. (84 dc)

Row 5: Ch 3, dc in each of next 11 sts, (2 dc, ch
2, 2 dc) in next ch-2 sp, dc in each of next 18 sts,
(2 dc, ch 2, 2 dc) in next ch-2 sp, dc in each of
next 24 sts, (2 dc, ch 2, 2 dc) in next ch-2 sp, dc
in each of next 18 sts, (2 dc, ch 2, 2 dc) in next
ch-2 sp, dc in each of last 12 sts, turn. (100 dc)

Row 6: Ch 1, sc in each of first 14 sts, sc in next
ch sp, for **armhole**, ch 5, sk next 22 sts, sc in
next ch sp, sc in each of next 28 sts, sc in next
ch sp, for **armhole**, ch 5, sk next 22 sts, sc in
next ch-2 sp, sc in each of last 14 sts, turn.
Fasten off. (70 sts and chs)

Row 7: Join (see Pattern Notes) with variegated
plum in first st, ch 3, (dc, ch 2, sc) in same st, [sk
next 2 sts or chs, **shell** (see Special Stitch) in next
st or ch] across, turn. (24 shells)

Row 8: Ch 3 (dc, ch 2, sc) in first st, shell in each
ch-2 sp across, turn.

Rep row 8 until desired length or 5 inches from
beg. At end of last row, **join** (see Pattern Notes)
in 3rd ch of beg ch-3. **Do not turn** at end of last
row.

LEG BANDS

Row 1: Ch 7, sc in last sc of 12th shell. Fasten off.

Rnd 2: Now working in rnds around 1 leg
opening, join white in 4th ch of ch-7, ch 2
(counts as first hdc), evenly sp 30 more hdc
around opening, join in 2nd ch of beg ch-2.
(31 hdc)

Rnds 3 & 4: Ch 2, hdc in each st around, join in
2nd ch of beg ch-2. Fasten off at end of last row.

Working on opposite side of ch-7, rep rnds 2–4 on
other leg opening.

SLEEVES
Rnd 1: Working around 1 armhole, join white with sc at bottom center of armhole, evenly sp 30 sc around armhole, join in beg sc. *(31 sc)*

Rnd 2: Ch 1, sc in each st around, join in beg sc. Fasten off.

Rep on other armhole opening.

Sew white buttons evenly sp to left back opening using sp between sts on right back for buttonholes.

Sew 1 dark purple flower to center front at lower edge of white section *(see photo)*. Sew 1 light purple flower to each side of dark purple flower.

NECK TRIM
Working in starting ch on opposite side of row 1, join variegated plum with sc in first ch, sc in each ch across with sc dec in next 3 sts in each corner. Fasten off.

BERET
Rnd 1: With size D hook and variegated plum, ch 5, join in beg ch to form ring, ch 3, 11 dc in ring, join in 3rd ch of beg ch-3. *(12 dc)*

Rnd 2: Ch 3, dc in same st, 2 dc in each st around, join in 3rd ch of beg ch-3. *(24 dc)*

Rnd 3: Ch 3, 2 dc in next st, [dc in next st, 2 dc in next st] around, join in 3rd ch of beg ch-3. *(36 dc)*

Rnd 4: Ch 3, dc in next st, 2 dc in next st, [dc in each of next 2 sts, 2 dc in next st] around, join in 3rd ch of beg ch-3. *(48 dc)*

Rnd 5: Ch 3, dc in each of next 2 sts, 2 dc in next st, [dc in each of next 3 sts, 2 dc in next st] around, join in 3rd ch of beg ch-3. *(60 dc)*

Rnd 6: Ch 3, dc in each of next 3 sts, 2 dc in next st, [dc in each of next 4 sts, 2 dc in next st] around, join in 3rd ch of beg ch-3. *(72 dc)*

Rnds 7 & 8: Ch 3, dc in each st around, join in 3rd ch of beg ch-3.

Rnd 9: Ch 3, dc in each of next 3 sts, **dc dec** *(see Stitch Guide)* in next 2 sts, [dc in each of next 4 sts, dc dec in next 2 sts] around, join in 3rd ch of beg ch-3. *(60 dc)*

Rnd 10: Ch 3, dc in each of next 2 sts, dc dec in next 2 sts, [dc in each of next 3 sts, dc dec in next 2 sts] around, join in 3rd ch of beg ch-3. Fasten off. *(48 dc)*

Rnd 11: Join white in first st, ch 2 *(counts as first hdc)*, hdc in each st around, join in 2nd ch of beg ch-2.

Rnds 12 & 13: Ch 2, hdc in each st around, join in 2nd ch of beg ch-2. Fasten off at end of last rnd.

CROCHET BUTTON
With white, ch 2, 12 sc in 2nd ch from hook, join in beg sc. Fasten off.

Sew Crochet Button to top of Beret.

Sew other dark purple flower to side of Beret close to last rnd.

BOOTIE
MAKE 2.
Rnd 1: With size C hook and white, ch 10, dc in 4th ch from hook *(first 3 chs count as first dc)*, dc in each of next 5 chs, 5 dc in last ch, working on opposite side of ch, dc in each of next 5 chs, 2 dc in last ch, join in 3rd ch of beg ch-3. *(19 dc)*

Rnd 2: Ch 3, dc in same st, dc in each of next 6 sts, 2 dc in each of next 5 sts, dc in each of next 6 sts, 2 dc in last st, join in 3rd ch of beg ch-3. *(26 dc)*

Rnd 3: Ch 3, dc in each st around, join in 3rd ch of beg ch-3.

Rnd 4: Ch 3, dc in each of next 8 sts, [dc dec in next 2 sts] 4 times, dc in each of last 9 sts, join in 3rd ch of beg ch-3. *(22 sts)*

Rnd 5: Ch 1, sc in each of first 7 sts, hdc in each of next 2 sts, [dc dec in next 2 sts] twice, hdc in each of next 2 sts, sc in each of last 7 sts, join in beg sc. *(20 sts)*

Rnds 6 & 7: Ch 3, dc in each st around, join in 3rd ch of beg ch-3. Fasten off at end of last rnd.

Rnd 8: Working this rnd in back lps, join variegated plum with sc in first st, sc in each st around, join in beg sc. Fasten off.

TIE
With variegated plum, ch for 12 inches. Fasten off.

Weave Tie through sts of rnd 6, tie ends into a bow at center front.■

Pink
Rose

EASY

FINISHED SIZES
Instructions given fit small 8-inch chubby doll; changes for medium 10-inch cloth doll and large 12-inch cloth doll are in [ ].

FINISHED MEASUREMENTS
Chest: 8½ inches *(small)* [8½ inches *(medium)*, 9 inches *(large)*]

MATERIALS
- Size 10 crochet cotton:
    350 yds medium pink
    60 yds dark pink
- Size steel crochet hook needed for size or size needed to obtain gauge
- Sewing needle
- ¼-inch buttons:
    2 white
- Ribbon:
    ¼-inch-wide: 2½ yds pink
    ³/₁₆-inch-wide: 2 yds pink
    ³/₁₆-inch-wide: 2 yds green
    ⅛-inch-wide: 1 yd dark pink

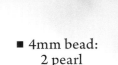

- 4mm bead:
    2 pearl
- Pink sewing thread
- Craft glue or hot-glue gun

GAUGE
Small & Medium Sizes: Size 7/1.65mm steel crochet hook: 15 dc = 2 inches; 8 dc rows = 2 inches

Large Size: Size 6/1.80 steel crochet hook: 13 dc = 2 inches; 7 dc rows = 2 inches

PATTERN NOTES
Join with slip stitch as indicated unless otherwise stated.

Chain-3 at beginning of row or round counts as first double crochet unless otherwise stated.

SPECIAL STITCHES

V-stitch (V-st): (Dc, ch 1, dc) in designated place.

Beginning V-stitch (Beg V-st): Ch 4 (counts as first dc and ch-1 sp), dc in same sp.

Shell: (2 dc, ch 2, 2 dc) in designated place.

INSTRUCTIONS
DRESS

Row 1 (RS): Starting at neck of bodice, with medium pink, ch 41, sc in 2nd ch from hook and in each ch across, turn. *(40 sc)*

Row 2: Ch 3 *(see Pattern Notes)*, dc in same st, dc in next st, [2 dc in next st, dc in next st] across, turn. *(60 dc)*

Row 3: Ch 3, dc in same st, dc in each of next 2 sts, [2 dc in next st, dc in each of next 2 sts] across, turn. *(80 dc)*

Row 4: Ch 3, dc in same st, dc in each of next 3 sts, [2 dc in next st, dc in each of next 3 sts] across, turn. *(100 dc)*

Row 5: Working this row in **back lps** *(see Stitch Guide)*, ch 3, dc in each of next 14 sts, for **armhole**, ch 5, sk next 20 sts, dc in each of next 30 sts, for **armhole**, ch 5, sk next 20 sts, dc in each of last 15 sts, turn. *(60 dc, 10 chs)*

Row 6: Ch 1, sc in each dc and ch across, turn. *(70 sc)*

Row 7: Ch 3, **V-st** *(see Special Stitches)* in next st, [sk next st, **shell** *(see Special Stitches)* in next st, sk next st, V-st in next st] across, turn. *(18 V-sts, 17 shells)*

Rows 8–16 [8–16, 8–18]: Ch 3, V-st in ch sp of first V-st, [shell in ch sp of next shell, V-st in ch sp of next V-st] across to last st, dc in last st, turn.

Row 17 [17, 19]: Ch 1, sc in first st, sc in ch sp of next V-st, [9 tr in ch sp of next shell, sc in ch sp of next V-st] across, sc in last st, **do not turn.** Fasten off. *(20 sc, 17 9-tr groups)*

Row 18 [18, 20]: Working in back lps, join dark pink with sc in first st, sc in each of next 9 sts, **sc dec** *(see Stitch Guide)* in next 3 sts, [sc in each of next 7 sts, sc dec in next 3 sts] 15 times, sc in each of last 10 sts. Fasten off.

NECK EDGING (OPTIONAL)

Working in starting ch on opposite side of row 1, with RS facing, join dark pink with sc in first ch, sc in each ch across. Fasten off.

SLEEVES

Rnd 1: Join medium pink with sc around last dc before ch-5 on 1 armhole in row 5, hdc around same dc, working in back lps across 20 sk sts, dc in each of next 8 dc, 2 dc in next st, dc in each of next 2 sts, 2 dc in next st, dc in each of next 8 dc, hdc around next dc in row 5, sc around same dc, working in opposite side of ch-5, sl st in each ch across, **join** *(see Pattern Notes)* in beg sc. *(31 sts)*

Rnd 2: Ch 1, sc in first st, hdc in next st, dc in each of next 22 sts, hdc in next st, sc in next st, sl st in each of next 5 sts, join in beg sc. *(31 sts)*

Rnd 3: Ch 1, sc in first st, hdc in next st, [**dc dec** *(see Stitch Guide)* in next 2 sts] 11 times, hdc in next st, sc in next st, sc in each of last 5 sl sts, join in beg sc. *(20 sts)*

Rnds 4 & 5: Ch 1, sc in each st around, join in beg sc. Fasten off at end of last rnd. *(20 sc)*

Rep on other armhole.

RIGHT PLACKET

Row 1: With WS facing, join medium pink with sc in bottom right-hand corner, working up to neck edge in ends of rows, evenly sp sc across to neck edge with 2 sc in end of each dc row, turn.

Row 2: Ch 1, sc in first st, for **buttonhole**, ch 3, sk next st, sc in each of next 6 sts, for **buttonhole**, ch 3, sk next st, sc in each st across. Fasten off.

LEFT PLACKET

Row 1: With WS facing, join with sc in top left-hand corner at neck edge, working down to hem edge in ends of rows, evenly sp sc across to hem edge with 2 sc in end of each dc row, turn.

Row 2: Ch 1, sc in each st across. Fasten off.

Sew buttons to Left Placket opposite buttonholes.

LARGE FLOWER
MAKE 2.
Cut a length of ¼-inch-wide ribbon 3½ inches long. With sewing needle and pink thread, gather 1 long edge of ribbon strand, pull tightly to form circle. Fold cut ends of ribbon to back and glue to secure. Glue 1 bead to center of Flower.

Glue 1 Large Flower to center front of Bodice and lay other aside.

EMBROIDERY
With pink and green ³/₁₆-inch-wide ribbon and **French knot** (*see illustration*) and **lazy-daisy stitch** (*see illustration*), embroider small flowers and rose buds around Large Flower (*see photo*).

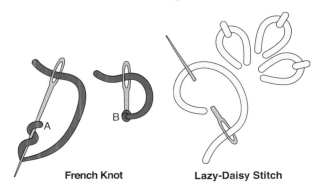

French Knot   **Lazy-Daisy Stitch**

BONNET
Rnd 1: With medium pink, ch 4, 11 dc in 4th ch from hook (*first 3 chs count as first dc*), **join** (*see Pattern Notes*) in 3rd ch of beg ch-3. (*12 dc*)

Rnd 2: Ch 3, dc in same st, 2 dc in each st around, join in 3rd ch of beg ch-3. (*24 dc*)

Rnd 3: Ch 3, 2 dc in next st, [dc in next st, 2 dc in next st] around, join in 3rd ch of beg ch-3. (*36 dc*)

Rnd 4: Ch 4 (*first ch-4 counts as first dc and ch-1 sp*), dc in same st, sk next st, shell in next st, sk next st, [V-st in next st, sk next st, shell in next st, sk next st] around, join in 3rd ch of beg ch-4. (*9 V-sts, 9 shells*)

Rnds 5–11: Sl st in next ch sp, **beg V-st** (*see Special Stitches*) in same sp, shell in ch sp of next shell, [V-st in ch sp of next V-st, shell in ch sp of next shell] around, join in 3rd ch of beg ch-4.

Rnd 12: Sl st in next ch sp, ch 1, sc in same sp, (tr {ch 1, tr} 6 times) in ch sp of next shell, [sc in ch sp of next V-st, (tr {ch 1, tr} 6 times) in ch sp of next shell] around, join in beg sc. Fasten off.

Rnd 13: Join dark pink in any sc, ch 3, [sl st in next ch-1 sp or next sc, ch 3] around, join in beg sl st. Fasten off.

Glue other Large Flower to 1 side of Bonnet and embroider same as Dress Embroidery.

Weave ¼-inch-wide ribbon through sts of rnd 9 on Bonnet, tie ends in bow below embroidery

SHOE
MAKE 2.
Rnd 1: With medium pink, ch 10, dc in 4th ch from hook (*first 3 chs count as first dc*), dc in each of next 5 chs, 5 dc in last ch, working on opposite side of ch, dc in each of next 5 chs, 2 dc in last ch, join in 3rd ch of beg ch-3. (*19 dc*)

Rnd 2: Ch 3, dc in same st, dc in each of next 6 sts, 2 dc in each of next 5 sts, dc in each of next 6 sts, 2 dc in last st, join in 3rd ch of beg ch-3. *(26 dc)*

Rnd 3: Ch 3, dc in each st around, join in 3rd ch of beg ch-3

Rnd 4: Ch 3, dc in each of next 8 sts, [dc dec in each of next 2 sts] 4 times, dc in each of last 9 sts, join in 3rd ch of beg ch-3. *(22 dc)*

Rnd 5: Ch 1, sc in each of first 9 sts, [sc dec in next 2 sts] twice, sc in each of last 9 sts, join in beg sc. Fasten off. *(20 sts)*

Weave 12 inches of ¼-inch-wide ribbon through stitches of row 4 at heel, pull ends even and tie around ankle with bow at front.

PANTS
Rnd 1: With dark pink, ch 60, sl st in first ch to form ring, ch 3, dc in each ch around, join in 3rd ch of beg ch-3. *(60 dc)*

Rnd 2: Ch 3, dc in each of next 4 sts, 2 dc in next st, [dc in each of next 5 sts, 2 dc in next st] around, join in 3rd ch of beg ch-3. *(70 dc)*

Rnds 3–4 [3–6, 3–9]: Ch 3, dc in each st around, join in 3rd ch of beg ch-3.

Rnd 5 [7, 10]: Ch 3, dc in each st around, join in 3rd ch of beg ch-3, ch 6, sk next 34 sts, sl st in next st, Fasten off.

LEGS
Rnd 1: Join in 4th ch of ch-6, ch 3, dc in next ch, dc dec in next ch and st, dc in each st across to one st before opposite side of ch-6, dc dec in next st and next ch, dc in each of last 2 chs, join in 3rd ch of beg ch-3. *(40 sts)*

Rnd 0 [2, 2]: Ch 3, dc in each st around, join in 3rd ch of beg ch-3.

Rnd 2 [3, 3]: Ch 1, **sc dec** *(see Stitch Guide)* in first 2 sts", [sc dec in next 2 sts] around, join in beg sc dec. *(20 sc dec)*

Rnds 3 & 4 [4 & 5, 4 & 5]: Ch 1, sc in each st around, join in beg sc. Fasten off at end of last row.

Working on opposite side of ch-6, rep on other Leg opening.

Cut ⅛-inch-wide ribbon in half, weave 1 strand ribbon through first rnd of sts on front and weave other strand ribbon through first rnd of sts on back.

Pull ribbon ends even, tie ends in bow at each side of Pants.

YARN
SKILL LEVEL

EASY

FINISHED SIZE
Fits 10-inch chubby doll

FINISHED MEASUREMENT
Chest: 10 inches

MATERIALS
- Super fine (fingering) yarn: 2 oz/350 yds/57g pink 100 yds dark pink
- Size C/2/2.75mm crochet hook or size needed to obtain gauge
- Sewing needle
- ½-inch buttons: 2 pink flower
- Ribbon:
  ⅜-inch-wide: 1½ yds dark pink
  ¼-inch-wide: 1 yd dark pink
  3⁄16-inch-wide: 1 yd pink
  3⁄16-inch-wide: 1 yd green
  ⅛-inch-wide: 1 yd dark pink
- 4mm beads: 2 pearl
- Pink sewing thread
- Craft glue or hot-glue gun

GAUGE
6 dc = 1 inch; 5 dc rows = 1½ inches

PATTERN NOTES
Join with slip stitch as indicated unless otherwise stated.

Chain-3 at beginning of row or round counts as first double crochet unless otherwise stated.

SPECIAL STITCHES

V-stitch (V-st): (Dc, ch 1, dc) in designated place.

Beginning V-stitch (Beg V-st): Ch 4 (counts as first dc and ch-1 sp), dc in same sp.

Shell: (2 dc, ch 2, 2 dc) in designated place.

INSTRUCTIONS
DRESS
Row 1 (RS): Starting at neck of bodice, with pink, ch 41, sc in 2nd ch from hook and in each ch across, turn. *(40 sc)*

Row 2: **Ch 3** *(see Pattern Notes)*, dc in same st, dc in next st, [2 dc in next st, dc in next st] across, turn. *(60 dc)*

Row 3: Ch 3, dc in same st, dc in each of next 2 sts, [2 dc in next st, dc in each of next 2 sts] across, turn. *(80 dc)*

Row 4: Ch 3, dc in same st, dc in each of next 3 sts, [2 dc in next st, dc in each of next 3 sts] across, turn. *(100 dc)*

Row 5: Working this row in **back lps** *(see Stitch Guide)*, ch 3, dc in each of next 14 sts, for **armhole**, ch 5, sk next 20 sts, dc in each of next 30 sts, for **armhole**, ch 5, sk next 20 sts, dc in each of last 15 sts, turn. *(60 dc, 10 chs)*

Row 6: Ch 1, sc in each dc and ch across, turn. *(70 sc)*

Row 7: Ch 3, **V-st** *(see Special Stitches)* in next st, [sk next st, **shell** *(see Special Stitches)* in next st, sk next st, V-st in next st] across, turn. *(18 V-sts, 17 shells)*

Rows 8–16: Ch 3, V-st in ch sp of first V-st, [shell in ch sp of next shell, V-st in ch sp of next V-st] across to last st, dc in last st, turn.

Row 17: Ch 1, sc in first st, sc in ch sp of next V-st, [9 tr in ch sp of next shell, sc in ch sp of next V-st] across, sc in last st, **do not turn**. Fasten off. *(20 sc, 17 9-tr groups)*

Row 18: Working in back lps, join dark pink with sc in first st, sc in each of next 9 sts, **sc dec** *(see Stitch Guide)* in next 3 sts, [sc in each of next 7 sts, sc dec in next 3 sts] 15 times, sc in each of last 10 sts. Fasten off.

NECK EDGING (OPTIONAL)
Working in starting ch on opposite side of row 1, with RS facing, join dark pink with sc in first ch, sc in each ch across. Fasten off.

SLEEVES
Rnd 1: Join pink with sc around last dc before ch-5 on 1 armhole in row 5, hdc around same dc, working in back lps across 20 sk sts, dc in each of next 8 dc, 2 dc in next st, dc in each of next 2 sts, 2 dc in next st, dc in each of next 8 dc, hdc around next dc in row 5, sc around same dc, working in opposite side of ch-5, sl st in each ch across, **join** *(see Pattern Notes)* in beg sc. *(31 sts)*

Rnd 2: Ch 1, sc in first st, hdc in next st, dc in each of next 22 sts, hdc in next st, sc in next st, sl st in each of next 5 sts, join in beg sc. *(31 sts)*

Rnd 3: Ch 1, sc in first st, hdc in next st, [**dc dec** *(see Stitch Guide)* in next 2 sts] 11 times, hdc in next st, sc in next st, sc in each of last 5 sl sts, join in beg sc. *(20 sts)*

Rnds 4 & 5: Ch 1, sc in each st around, join in beg sc. Fasten off at end of last rnd. *(20 sc)*

Rep on other armhole.

RIGHT PLACKET
Row 1: With WS facing, join medium pink with sc in bottom right-hand corner, working up to neck edge in ends of rows, evenly sp sc across to neck edge with 2 sc in end of each dc row, turn.

Row 2: Ch 1, sc in first st, for **buttonhole**, ch 3, sk next st, sc in each of next 6 sts, for **buttonhole**, ch 3, sk next st, sc in each st across. Fasten off.

LEFT PLACKET
Row 1: With WS facing, join with sc in top left-hand corner at neck edge, working down to hem edge in ends of rows, evenly sp sc across to hem edge with 2 sc in end of each dc row, turn.

Row 2: Ch 1, sc in each st across. Fasten off.

Sew buttons to Left Placket opposite buttonholes.

LARGE FLOWER
MAKE 2.

Cut a length of ¼-inch-wide dark pink ribbon 3½ inches long. With sewing needle and pink thread, gather 1 long edge of ribbon strand, pull tightly to form circle. Fold cut ends of ribbon to back and glue to secure. Glue 1 bead to center of Flower.

Glue 1 Large Flower to center front of Bodice and lay other aside.

EMBROIDERY

With pink and green ³/₁₆-inch-wide ribbon and **French knot** (*see illustration*) and **lazy-daisy stitch** (*see illustration*), embroider small flowers and rose buds around Large Flower (*see photo*).

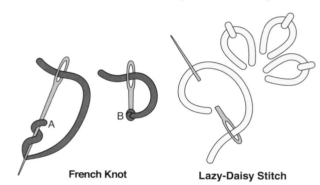

French Knot   Lazy-Daisy Stitch

BONNET

Rnd 1: With pink, ch 4, 11 dc in 4th ch from hook (*first 3 chs count as first dc*), join in 3rd ch of beg ch-3. (*12 dc*)

Rnd 2: Ch 3, dc in same st, 2 dc in each st around, join in 3rd ch of beg ch-3. (*24 dc*)

Rnd 3: Ch 3, 2 dc in next st, [dc in next st, 2 dc in next st] around, join in 3rd ch of beg ch-3. (*36 dc*)

Rnd 4: Ch 4 (*first ch-4 counts as first dc and ch-1 sp*), dc in same st, sk next st, shell in next st, sk next st, [V-st in next st, sk next st, shell in next st, sk next st] around, join in 3rd ch of beg ch-4. (*9 V-sts, 9 shells*)

Rnds 5–11: Sl st in next ch sp, **beg V-st** (*see Special Stitches*) in same sp, shell in ch sp of next shell, [V-st in ch sp of next V-st, shell in ch sp of next shell] around, join in 3rd ch of beg ch-4.

Rnd 12: Sl st in next ch sp, ch 1, sc in same sp, (tr {ch 1, tr} 6 times) in ch sp of next shell, [sc in ch sp of next V-st, (tr, {ch 1, tr} 6 times) in ch sp of next shell] around, join in beg sc. Fasten off.

Rnd 13: Join dark pink in any sc, ch 3, [sl st in next ch-1 sp or next sc, ch 3] around, join in beg sc. Fasten off.

Glue other Large Flower to 1 side of Bonnet and embroider same as Dress Embroidery.

Weave ³/₈-inch-wide dark pink ribbon through sts of rnd 9 on Bonnet, tie ends in bow below embroidery.

SHOE
MAKE 2.

Rnd 1: With medium pink, ch 10, dc in 4th ch from hook (*first 3 chs count as first dc*), dc in each of next 5 chs, 5 dc in last ch, working on opposite side of ch, dc in each of next 5 chs, 2 dc in last ch, join in 3rd ch of beg ch-3. (*19 dc*)

Rnd 2: Ch 3, dc in same st, dc in each of next 6 sts, 2 dc in each of next 5 sts, dc in each of next 6 sts, 2 dc in last st, join in 3rd ch of beg ch-3. (*26 dc*)

Rnd 3: Ch 3, dc in each st around, join in 3rd ch of beg ch-3

Rnd 4: Ch 3, dc in each of next 8 sts, [dc dec in each of next 2 sts] 4 times, dc in each of last 9 sts, join in 3rd ch of beg ch-3. (*22 dc*)

Rnd 5: Ch 1, sc in each of first 9 sts, [sc dec in next 2 sts] twice, sc in each of last 9 sts, join in beg sc. Fasten off. (*20 sts*)

Weave 12 inches of ¼-inch-wide dark pink ribbon through stitches of row 4 at heel, pull ends even and tie around ankle with bow at front.

PANTS

Rnd 1: With dark pink, ch 60, sl st in first ch to form ring, ch 3, dc in each ch around, join in 3rd ch of beg ch-3. (*60 dc*)

Rnd 2: Ch 3, dc in each of next 4 sts, 2 dc in next st, [dc in each of next 5 sts, 2 dc in next st] around, join in 3rd ch of beg ch-3. *(70 dc)*

Rnds 3 & 4: Ch 3, dc in each st around, join in 3rd ch of beg ch-3.

Rnd 5: Ch 3, dc in each st around, join in 3rd ch of beg ch-3, ch 6 sk next 34 sts, sl st in next st. Fasten off.

LEGS

Rnd 1: Join in 4th ch of ch-6, ch 3, dc in next ch, dc dec in next ch and st, dc in each st across to one st before opposite side of ch-6, dc dec in next st and next ch, dc in each of last 2 chs, join in 3rd ch of beg ch 3. *(40 sts)*

Rnd 2: Ch 1, **sc dec** *(see Stitch Guide)* in first 2 sts, [sc dec in next 2 sts] around, join in beg sc dec. *(20 sc dec)*

Rnd 3: Ch 1, sc in each st around, join in beg sc. Fasten off.

Working on opposite side of ch-6, rep on other Leg opening.

Cut ⅛-inch-wide dark pink ribbon in half, weave 1 strand ribbon through first rnd of sts on front and weave other strand ribbon through first rnd of sts on back.

Pull ribbon ends even, tie ends in bow at each side of Pants.■

STITCH GUIDE

STITCH ABBREVIATIONS

beg	begin/begins/beginning
bpdc	back post double crochet
bpsc	back post single crochet
bptr	back post treble crochet
CC	contrasting color
ch(s)	chain(s)
ch-	refers to chain or space previously made (i.e., ch-1 space)
ch sp(s)	chain space(s)
cl(s)	cluster(s)
cm	centimeter(s)
dc	double crochet (singular/plural)
dc dec	double crochet 2 or more stitches together, as indicated
dec	decrease/decreases/decreasing
dtr	double treble crochet
ext	extended
fpdc	front post double crochet
fpsc	front post single crochet
fptr	front post treble crochet
g	gram(s)
hdc	half double crochet
hdc dec	half double crochet 2 or more stitches together, as indicated
inc	increase/increases/increasing
lp(s)	loop(s)
MC	main color
mm	millimeter(s)
oz	ounce(s)
pc	popcorn(s)
rem	remain/remains/remaining
rep(s)	repeat(s)
rnd(s)	round(s)
RS	right side
sc	single crochet (singular/plural)
sc dec	single crochet 2 or more stitches together, as indicated
sk	skip/skipped/skipping
sl st(s)	slip stitch(es)
sp(s)	space(s)/spaced
st(s)	stitch(es)
tog	together
tr	treble crochet
trtr	triple treble
WS	wrong side
yd(s)	yard(s)
yo	yarn over

YARN CONVERSION

OUNCES TO GRAMS		GRAMS TO OUNCES	
1	28.4	25	⅞
2	56.7	40	1⅔
3	85.0	50	1¾
4	113.4	100	3½

UNITED STATES		UNITED KINGDOM
sl st (slip stitch)	=	sc (single crochet)
sc (single crochet)	=	dc (double crochet)
hdc (half double crochet)	=	htr (half treble crochet)
dc (double crochet)	=	tr (treble crochet)
tr (treble crochet)	=	dtr (double treble crochet)
dtr (double treble crochet)	=	ttr (triple treble crochet)
skip	=	miss

Reverse Single Crochet (reverse sc): Ch 1. Skip first st. [Working from left to right, insert hook in next st from front to back, draw up lp on hook, yo, and draw through both lps on hook.]

Chain (ch): Yo, pull through lp on hook.

Single crochet (sc): Insert hook in st, yo, pull through st, yo, pull through both lps on hook.

Double crochet (dc): Yo, insert hook in st, yo, pull through st, [yo, pull through 2 lps] twice.

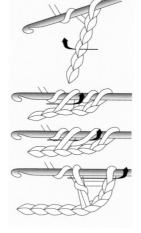

Front loop (front lp) Back loop (back lp)

Front Loop   Back Loop

Front post stitch (fp): Back post stitch (bp): When working post st, insert hook from right to left around post st on previous row.

Back   Front

Post of Stitch

Half double crochet (hdc): Yo, insert hook in st, yo, pull through st, yo, pull through all 3 lps on hook.

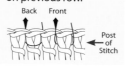

Double treble crochet (dtr): Yo 3 times, insert hook in st, yo, pull through st, [yo, pull through 2 lps] 4 times.

Slip stitch (sl st): Insert hook in st, pull through both lps on hook.

Chain Color Change (ch color change) Yo with new color, draw through last lp on hook.

Double Crochet Color Change (dc color change) Drop first color, yo with new color, draw through last 2 lps of st.

Treble crochet (tr): Yo twice, insert hook in st, yo, pull through st, [yo, pull through 2 lps] 3 times.

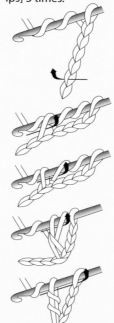

Single crochet decrease (sc dec): (Insert hook, yo, draw lp through) in each of the sts indicated, yo, draw through all lps on hook.

Example of 2-sc dec

Half double crochet decrease (hdc dec): (Yo, insert hook, yo, draw lp through) in each of the sts indicated, yo, draw through all lps on hook.

Example of 2-hdc dec

Double crochet decrease (dc dec): Yo, insert hook, yo, draw loop through, draw through 2 lps on hook) in each of the sts indicated, yo, draw through all lps on hook.

Example of 2-dc dec

Treble crochet decrease (tr dec): Holding back last lp of each st, tr in each of the sts indicated, yo, pull through all lps on hook.

Example of 2-tr dec

Metric
Conversion
Charts

METRIC CONVERSIONS

yards	x	.9144	=	metres (m)
yards	x	91.44	=	centimetres (cm)
inches	x	2.54	=	centimetres (cm)
inches	x	25.40	=	millimetres (mm)
inches	x	.0254	=	metres (m)

centimetres	x	.3937	=	inches
metres	x	1.0936	=	yards

INCHES INTO MILLIMETRES & CENTIMETRES (Rounded off slightly)

inches	mm	cm	inches	cm	inches	cm	inches	cm
1/8	3	0.3	5	12.5	21	53.5	38	96.5
1/4	6	0.6	5 1/2	14	22	56	39	99
3/8	10	1	6	15	23	58.5	40	101.5
1/2	13	1.3	7	18	24	61	41	104
5/8	15	1.5	8	20.5	25	63.5	42	106.5
3/4	20	2	9	23	26	66	43	109
7/8	22	2.2	10	25.5	27	68.5	44	112
1	25	2.5	11	28	28	71	45	114.5
1 1/4	32	3.2	12	30.5	29	73.5	46	117
1 1/2	38	3.8	13	33	30	76	47	119.5
1 3/4	45	4.5	14	35.5	31	79	48	122
2	50	5	15	38	32	81.5	49	124.5
2 1/2	65	6.5	16	40.5	33	84	50	127
3	75	7.5	17	43	34	86.5		
3 1/2	90	9	18	46	35	89		
4	100	10	19	48.5	36	91.5		
4 1/2	115	11.5	20	51	37	94		

KNITTING NEEDLES CONVERSION CHART

Canada/U.S.	0	1	2	3	4	5	6	7	8	9	10	10½	11	13	15
Metric (mm)	2	2¼	2¾	3¼	3½	3¾	4	4½	5	5½	6	6½	8	9	10

CROCHET HOOKS CONVERSION CHART

Canada/U.S.	1/B	2/C	3/D	4/E	5/F	6/G	8/H	9/I	10/J	10½/K	N
Metric (mm)	2.25	2.75	3.25	3.5	3.75	4.25	5	5.5	6	6.5	9.0

RETAIL STORES: If you would like to carry this pattern book or any other DRG publications, visit DRGwholesale.com

Every effort has been made to ensure that the instructions in this publication are complete and accurate.
We cannot, however, take responsibility for human error, typographical mistakes or variations in individual work.
Please visit AnniesCustomerCare.com to check for pattern updates.

ISBN: 978-1-59635-334-3

1 2 3 4 5 6 7 8 9